T0413963

EVADING THE ERUPTION

by Charlie Ogden &
Sam Thompson

BEARPORT
PUBLISHING

Minneapolis, Minnesota

Credits
Images are courtesy of Shutterstock.com. With thanks to Getty Images, Thinkstock Photo, and iStockphoto. Recurring images – benchart, Anastasiia Veretennikova, Francois Poirier, Slay, PrimeMockup, Panuwach, Net Vector. Cover – Zerbor, jakkapan, Terablete. 4–5 – Roberto Destarac Photo, Deni_Sugandi. 6–7 – 300dpi, EricLiu08, Jagoush. 8–9 – cigdem, Aldona Griskeviciene. 10–11 – Stock-Asso, Simone Migliaro, Frame Stock Footage. 12–13 – Karramba Production, LukaKikina. 14Ð15 – 4zevar, Alexander Piragis, Ammit Jack, Galyna Andrushko. 16–17 – 4zevar, Markus Mainka, Shark_749. 18–19 – frozenbunn, Kostikova Natalia, Rebellion Works. 20–21 – ahmad zikri, BLUR LIFE 1975. 22–23 – Hadrian, Igor Hotinsky. 24–25 – Anna Violet, Good Luck Photo, Krakenimages.com, TORWAISTUDIO. 26–27 – ja-aljona, Thomas Dekiere. 28–29 – Just dance, Vladimir Konstantinov.

Bearport Publishing Company Product Development Team
President: Jen Jenson; Director of Product Development: Spencer Brinker; Managing Editor: Allison Juda; Associate Editor: Naomi Reich; Associate Editor: Tiana Tran; Art Director: Colin O'Dea; Designer: Elena Klinkner; Designer: Kayla Eggert; Product Development Assistant: Owen Hamlin

Library of Congress Cataloging-in-Publication Data is available at www.loc.gov or upon request from the publisher.

ISBN: 979-8-88916-592-7 (hardcover)
ISBN: 979-8-88916-597-2 (paperback)
ISBN: 979-8-88916-601-6 (ebook)

For more information, write to Bearport Publishing, 5357 Penn Avenue South, Minneapolis, MN 55419.

CONTENTS

KABOOM!

How would you feel if the ground began to rumble? Then, what if you heard a loud boom?

If you don't like the heat, be warned . . .

IT'S AN ERUPTION!

What would you do if a **volcano** erupted?

It is time to become an eruption survival **expert.**

A SUPERVOLCANO

Volcanoes are very dangerous, yet we build towns and cities near them.

Imagine a volcano. Then, think of something 1,000 times bigger. That's a supervolcano!

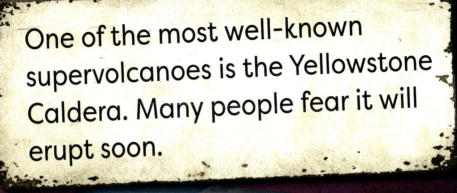

One of the most well-known supervolcanoes is the Yellowstone Caldera. Many people fear it will erupt soon.

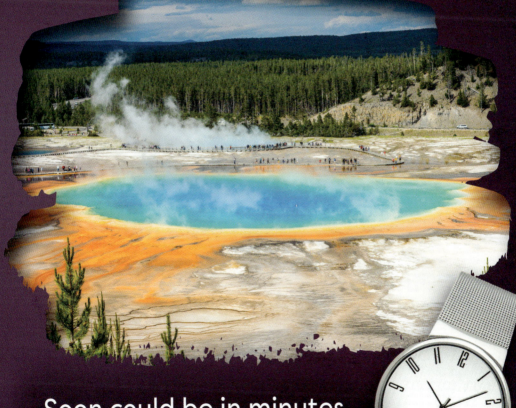

Soon could be in minutes, years, or even **centuries**. Nobody knows for sure.

SUPER SCIENCE

Learning about volcanoes will help you survive a volcanic eruption.

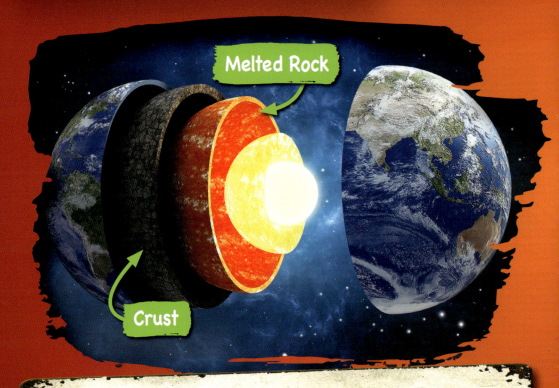

Melted Rock

Crust

Earth is made up of many layers. The outer layer is called the **crust**. Below the crust is very hot melted rock.

The melted rock in the ground is called magma. Over time, **pressure** can build up. This forces the magma up and out of volcanoes. Once magma flows onto land, it is called lava.

Lava

Magma

ROYALLY RUMBLED

There are always warning signs before a volcanic eruption.

The ground might shake beneath you. This is called an earthquake.

Check the news if you feel an earthquake.
Go on the internet or switch on the TV.

An earthquake might **trigger** a
supervolcano. You will need to be ready.

GET TO SAFETY

Keep your cool.
Head away
from danger.

Volcano

Hazard zone

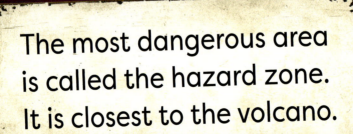

The most dangerous area
is called the hazard zone.
It is closest to the volcano.

Ash and rock will fall from the sky there. Soon, the land will be buried under ash.

Find your family. **Evacuate** the area to survive.

You must find a good place to hide. Indoors is your best option. Find a house and get upstairs.

FIND SHELTER

If there is no shelter, then get to higher ground instead.

Find a mountain and start climbing. The higher you can get, the better.

YOUR
SURVIVAL KIT

Grab supplies on your way to safety.

Find some canned food from a nearby store. It lasts for a long time.

Pack bottled water. Ash from the eruption will make tap water dirty.

Keep an eye on the news. It will tell you when the water is safe to drink again.

Are you in a house? Look through the cupboards. See if you can find a first aid kit.

What else should you look for? Maybe you can find a radio to listen to the news.

Soon, ash will block the sunlight. That means it will be dark all the time.

Find a flashlight and batteries.

ALL PYRO,
NO PARTY

Watch out for pyroclastic flows. These are clouds of ash, gases, and pieces of rock that can come out of volcanoes.

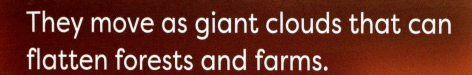

They move as giant clouds that can flatten forests and farms.

If you are outside, watch out for flying rocks.

These steps could help you survive.

- Hide behind walls or rocks.

- Crouch down and face away from the volcano.

- Protect your head.

The ash will make the air unsafe to breathe. Keep all windows and doors closed. Do not open them unless you have to.

Are there any gaps around your doors? Cover them with **damp** towels to keep the ash out.

One day, you might run out of supplies. But it's not safe to breathe outside.

Do not go out unless you have a special mask to stop you from breathing in ash. Make sure your skin is fully covered.

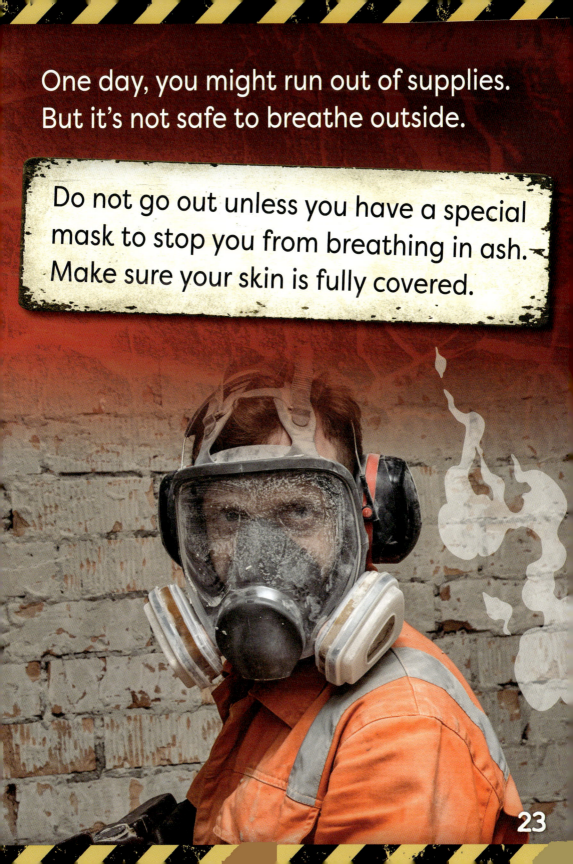

It is not just ash that can cause problems. Volcanic gases in the air can be deadly, too.

Carbon dioxide is a gas that is usually harmless. We breathe it out. But taking in a lot of this gas can be very dangerous.

Other volcanic gases smell like rotten eggs. *Gross!*

Get away from any bad smells.

FROM ONE DISASTER TO ANOTHER

The supervolcano blast won't be the end of the disaster.

Landslides happen when large areas of ground get loose. The earth slides down cliffs and the sides of mountains. It crushes anything in its path.

Avoid riverbanks and valleys. Protect your head and stay on the lookout for anything falling.

A FREEZING CHANGE

The eruption of a supervolcano will change the planet.

Clouds from the volcano will block out daylight. Without the sun, it will be cold and dark everywhere.

Get ready to wait out the big freeze.
Find blankets and sweaters to stay warm.

It could take years before things
get back to normal.

THE DISASTER
CHECKLIST

How can you evade the eruption?

- ✓ Learn about volcanoes.

- ✓ Check the news.

- ✓ Leave the hazard zone.

- ✓ Find shelter or higher ground.

- ✓ Gather supplies.

- ✓ Close doors and windows.

- ✓ Expect more disasters.

GLOSSARY

centuries units of one hundred years

crust the hard outer layer of Earth

damp a little wet

evacuate to move away from a dangerous area

expert someone who knows a lot about a subject

pressure the force made when something presses on something else

trigger to set off something

volcano a mountain that can erupt to let out hot, melted rock

INDEX

READ MORE

Collins, Ailynn. *Can You Survive the Great San Francisco Earthquake? An Interactive History Adventure (You Choose: Disasters in History).* North Mankato, MN: Capstone Press, 2022.

Mitchell, K. S. *Avalanches and Landslides (Severe Weather).* Mendota Heights, MN: Apex Editions, 2023.

LEARN MORE ONLINE

1. Go to **www.factsurfer.com** or scan the QR code below.

2. Enter "**Evading Eruption**" into the search box.

3. Click on the cover of this book to see a list of websites.